Written by
Máire de Paor

Early Irish Art

Published by
The Department of Foreign Affairs, Dublin, Ireland

Dublin 1979, reprinted 1983

D0129209

Máire de Paor was born in Buncrana, Co. Donegal and educated there and at U.C.D. where she received her Ph.D. in archaeology. She was a member of staff in the Dept. of Archaeology for twelve years and has also taught in Trinity College, Dublin, St Patrick's College, Maynooth, University College, Cork and Queen's College, New York. She has carried out excavations at many sites in Ireland and on Celtic sites in Portugal. Specialising in Early Christian and Viking periods in Irish art, she has written numerous articles and is co-author, with her husband, Liam de Paor of Early Christian Ireland. *She is a member of the Council of the Royal Irish Academy and of the Arts Council. At present she is a researcher for Radio Telefís Éireann for educational and cultural programmes.*

ISBN 0 906404 03 7

Design by Bill Murphy, MSIA, FIBD, MSDI
Printed by Wood-Printcraft, Dublin, Ireland

Contents

5 **Acknowledgements**

7 **Introduction**

9 **Megalithic Art**

13 **The Art of the Bronze Age**

17 **Early Celtic Art**

23 **Roman Influence**

27 **The Golden Age**

39 **The Viking Impact**

47 **Romanesque**

53 **Gothic**

57 **Bibliography**

Acknowledgements

Except where otherwise stated, all the portable objects mentioned in the text are in the National Museum of Ireland. We are grateful to the authorities of the National Museum for supplying photographs of these objects and for permission to reproduce them. We wish to thank the Board of Trinity College, Dublin for permission to publish photographs of the Books of Durrow and Kells and the Green Studio for supplying them. Thanks are due to the Royal Irish Academy for the photograph of the *Cathach* manuscript and to the Hi storisk Museum, Bergen, for Plate 30 (Photograph: Ann-Mari Olsen).
We are grateful to the Commissioners of Public Works for permission to reproduce photographs of the monuments in their care and for supplying all the photographs here produced. The photograph of the Boa Island figure (Plate 19) was supplied by the Northern Ireland Tourist Board. Plate 34, from the St Gall Gospels was supplied by the Cathedral Library, St Gall, and the photograph of the Emly Shrine (Plate 25) was supplied by The Boston Museum of Fine Arts.

Introduction

Early Irish art was created in a milieu very different from that which produced what, in modern times, we distinguish as works of art. In the pre-Norman period in particular, most works, for example, are unsigned: the artists remain anonymous. The distinction between what is a work of art and what is a work of utility is rarely clear; to a great extent we are dealing with 'applied art'.

Much of the study of objects and ornaments has been carried out in the field of archaeology, and indeed many of the objects themselves have come to light through archaeological excavation. We have a range of material from everyday utilitarian objects, which may be so shaped, designed and finished that we can regard them as works of art in their own right to splendid creations in which the artistic purpose, in our understanding of the words, is in no doubt, as for example in the entrance stone at Newgrange or in the glittering relief ornament and moulding of the Broighter collar. But even with these, the artists' names remain unknown. Other stones were carved, or weapons and ornaments cast for religious or military or display purposes. The craftsmen, meeting the demands of a traditional society, obeying the rules of style and fashion, could create works of great beauty and even originality.

Perhaps the prevailing characteristics throughout this long period of Irish art were a passion for abstraction and stylisation, an interest in the symbol rather than the naturalistic depiction of nature or human beings, a love of pattern within a discipline which seldom allowed deterioration into monotony. The artist, particularly in the early Christian period, was eclectic in his choice of models, borrowing ideas and techniques from many sources in Europe and even father afield. But right up to and including the Romanesque period, he made these borrowings his own, producing something uniquely Irish and original.

It was only when the whole Irish way of life, the whole structure of society, was broken up by successive settlements of newcomers in the Norman and Tudor periods that this native originality faded, and Irish art became a part of the European scene.

Megalithic Art

1 *Stone in passage of western tomb in large mound at Knowth, Co. Meath. The carving may represent a human figure. Neolithic.*

2 *Decorated kerb-stone from large passage-grave at Knowth, Co. Meath. Neolithic.*

Megalithic Art

The first farmers who settled in Ireland, sometime before 3,000 BC, arrived here from the Mediterranean, bringing with them the skills of crop-growing, domestication of animals and a characteristic round-bottomed hand-made pottery. They came by the Atlantic sea-route and made their way northwards and westwards by way of Spain and Western France, and their most characteristic monuments are the great megalithic tombs which can be found in all these areas. The urban civilisation from which they sprang was left behind in the Mediterranean lands, but the great stone tombs for collective burial are the earliest works of architecture which survive in France, Britain and Ireland.

The most elaborate of these tombs and the closest to Spanish and Breton prototypes are the passage-graves — large round mounds or cairns of stone, covering a burial chamber or chambers approached by a passage. These are grouped in cemeteries, probably preserving the memory of a city culture, and in Ireland such cemeteries can be found in the Boyne Valley, the Dublin-Wicklow mountains, the Lough Crew Hills, Co. Meath, and at Carrowmore and Carrowkeel, Co. Sligo.

Two of these cemeteries are notable for the decoration which appears carved on the stones — that of the Boyne, including the magnificent tombs at Newgrange, Dowth and Knowth and that of Lough

2

Megalithic Art

3 Crew, both in Co. Meath. There are a few examples of carving in the Dublin-Wicklow group but no ornament occurs on the Sligo tombs. Outside Ireland, carvings are found in Brittany and in Wales but in Iberia the tombs themselves are undecorated. There, however, the grave goods accompanying the burials include small plaques or cylinders decorated with stylised representations of the female form in a very distinctive linear style. Even more stylised representations occur on pottery vessels.

The art in Ireland is purely abstract — spirals, zig-zags, lozenges, meanders — and the designs are found on the tomb walls, on lintels and kerb-stones and even on the roofing-stones of chambers. The commonest technique used in the carving is a picking of the stone surface giving a stippled effect to the ornament. Experiment has shown that this was achieved by using a stone point, quartz or flint, because of course this was before the knowledge of metal in Ireland. Many undecorated stones are dressed with the same technique. The picking varies from fine to coarse. Sometimes the actual ornament is picked out, sometimes (as on the entrance stone at Newgrange) the background is pocked so that the design stands out in relief.

Spirals are common in Ireland but rare elsewhere. They are used to great effect at Newgrange combined in various forms. Lozenges and chevrons and triangles are the commonest of the rectilinear designs. Sometimes spirals and lozenges are combined to give the effect of eyes and nose — the Irish version of the Breton *occuli* design. Anthropomorphic designs are found at Fourknocks and Knowth. Concentric circles, cartouches or shield-shaped motifs, groups of arcs or pendant semi-circles and serpentine designs all occur. A great variety of motifs has been revealed by recent excavations at Knowth. As at Newgrange there is close harmony between art and architecture, the kerb-stones and the innermost stones of the chamber being highly decorated. The style of ornament at Lough Crew (which resembles some of the Dowth carvings) is more minute, less related to tomb architecture and less pervasive over the surface of the stones. Sun-flower designs, rayed

Megalithic Art

3 *Stone from chamber of passage-grave at Fourknocks, Co. Meath, showing stylised human face. Neolithic.*

4 *Carved kerb-stone at entrance to passage-grave Newgrange, Co. Meath with spiral and lozenge designs. Neolithic.*

4

Megalithic Art

circles and shield motifs are the most characteristic forms. Chevrons and zig-zags are used most strikingly at Fourknocks, Co. Meath, one of the most interesting of the decorated tombs.

This wholly abstract art obviously had a deeply felt religious significance. The compositions and forms once had a meaning now lost to us. The disintegrated faces and forms may relate to the representations found on idols in Iberia, which represent the mother-goddess or death-goddess of the Mediterranean. We do not know if the builders of the Irish tombs still worshipped her, or if she herself as well as her features had been forgotten. The movements of the sun obviously had a significance for the megalith builders as is clear from some of the architectural features of the tombs. Whatever their beliefs, some powerful faith impelled these early Irishmen to construct astonishingly elaborate monuments and to devote endless patience and care to carving the great stones with this mysterious art.

The Art of the Bronze Age

5 *Decorated stone from passage of Cairn T, Lough Crew, Co. Meath with cup-and-circle, sunflower, and rayed-circle ornament. Neolithic.*

6 *Vase Food Vessel from Tankardstown, Co. Louth, with hatched ornament. Early Bronze Age.*

7 *Riveted sheet-bronze cauldron, Castlederg, Co. Tyrone. Late Bronze Age.*

The knowledge and use of metal came to northern and western Europe from the Mediterranean and reached Ireland relatively early. This was probably partly due to Ireland's geographical position but even more to her natural resources of copper and gold which attracted early prospectors. Some time in the neighbourhood of 2,000 BC, people were manufacturing objects of metal in Ireland; of copper or gold first, later on of bronze, an alloy of copper and tin which was harder and more serviceable than copper. The tin used in Ireland was probably imported from Cornwall, a rich source of tin, although some small amounts may have been obtained here. Overseas trade was one of the features of the Irish Early Bronze Age and for a time Irish metalworkers supplied markets in Britain and the Continent.

A series of rock carvings, mainly with curvilinear designs, concentric circles, cup and ring marks and some labyrinthine patterns occur, mainly in the south-west of the country in Cork and Kerry. These are found on natural rock-surfaces and have been compared to similar rock art in Galicia. It is possible that they were introduced by prospectors for metal coming from northern Spain and Portugal and there may also be some overlap with the art of the passage graves. However, with these exceptions, most of the art which survives from the Irish Bronze Age is on objects of metal.

It is an applied art appearing on objects of utility or personal adornment. Simple linear designs — arrangements of triangles and chevrons, alternation of hatched and unhatched spaces, herring-bone designs and criss-cross hatching — appear on early metal objects such as flat axe-heads, knives and daggers and on gold ornaments. The designs also appear on the surface of the hand-made pottery of the period — Beakers and Food Vessels — and quite likely come from this source. Some of the patterns may derive from the magical or religious art of the megalithic tombs. At a later stage in the Bronze Age, many of the surface ornaments on metal objects are 'skeuomorphic', repeating as ornament forms which once had been utilitarian. For instance, the cast-cable ornament on some

The Art of the Bronze Age

8 socketed axes derives from the cord binding which had helped to secure earlier types of axe-head to the shaft.

Within this comparatively narrow range, the goldsmiths and bronzesmiths of the Bronze Age produced striking and beautiful objects. The earlier period when Ireland was exporting metal products and when there was a demand for Irish gold has been termed 'Ireland's first Golden Age'. At this time the most outstanding objects in gold were made — the lunulae. These are crescent-shaped sheets of beaten gold with fastenings at the narrow terminals, designed to be worn around the neck or breast. The surface of the hammered gold was decorated with incised linear geometric patterns confined mainly to the horns of the crescent and the rims. The motifs used and the arrangement of the ornament is similar to the decoration and lay-out of multiple-strand jet necklaces found mainly in Scotland. They seem to be Irish versions of a type of neck-ornament in different media known from various areas of Europe — copper on the Continent, amber in southern Britain, jet in northern Britain. Over sixty gold lunulae have been found in Ireland, others, probably exports, have been found in Scotland, Wales and Cornwall and along the coastal areas of the Continent, chiefly in France but extending along the North Sea to Denmark. Small ornamented discs of thin sheet gold were made in Ireland at the same period. They are often found in pairs and have two small perforations near the centre for attaching them to some material Each disc has in its centre a repoussé cruciform design enclosed in concentric circles with chevrons or dots. Similar cross motifs are found on the bottom of Food Vessels. These are known as sun-discs and possibily may have been associated with the cult of the sun. Similar gold discs continued to be made in the later Bronze Age and others resembling them were made in the Baltic area. Ear-rings shaped like shallow baskets or panniers were also made out of thin sheet gold in the Early Bronze Age.

Gold continued to be plentiful in Ireland throughout the Bronze Age but some of the later objects achieved their effect by their form alone without the aid of surface ornament. This is particularly true of

The Art of the Bronze Age

9
10

8 *Gold lunula or neck ornament with engraved abstract patterns, from Dunfierth, Co. Meath. Early Bronze Age.*

9 *Gold ribbon torque found near Belfast, Co. Antrim. Late Bronze Age.*

10 *Ribbed gold gorget or collar from Gleninsheen, Co. Clare. Late Bronze Age.*

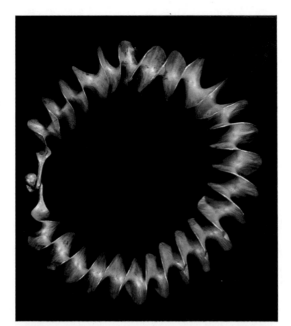

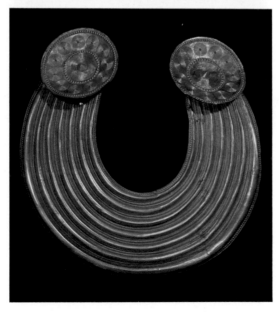

the torques, made, as their name implies, from twisting ribbons of gold. The simplest form of torque was made by beating out a bar of gold of square section or more rarely a ribbon of gold, and then twisting it all along its length. It was then curved around into a circlet which fastened at the free end with simple hooked clasps or later with reflexed terminals. Earrings, bracelets, girdles, probably ceremonial, and, most commonly, neck-rings, were made in this manner. The inspiration for the form seems to have been from Scandinavia but there the ornaments were made of bronze. More elaborate effects were produced by first of all hammering the rod of gold into flanges to give a cross-section in the form of a Greek cross and then twisting it; this gave a glittering, faceted appearance.

A great wealth and diversity of personal ornament mainly in gold is known from the Late Bronze Age, particularly in the period between 800 and 600 BC, and many of the types had Scandinavian connections. Elegant bracelets of smooth curved gold with simple extended terminals were made as well as more unusual ribbed armlets. Gold objects known as dress-fasteners are pinless versions of the bronze fibulae of northern Europe. These are in the form of a tube, curved into a bow which joins two flaring trumpet-shaped terminals, which often carry an ornament of concentric circles. They would have been used in the manner of a modern cuff-link to join two sides of a cloak or heavy garment. Smaller, rather similar objects may have been sleeve fasteners. Ornamental rivets and groups of concentric circles also decorate pins with large circular heads, placed at right angles to the shank. These are usually made of bronze and are known as sunflower pins.

Perhaps the most technically accomplished products of this period are the hair-rings or lock-rings. These are biconical — thin sheets of metal, joined together by a rounded binding strip. A continuous series of tiny parallel grooves covers the surface of the cones. In some cases the grooves were made by laying fine wires side by side and then soldering them together — work of extraordinary fineness.

The Art of the Bronze Age

A number of these hair-rings have been found in the area round the mouth of the Shannon and the same location has produced almost all of the gold gorgets — the most striking of all Irish Bronze Age ornaments. These are massive crescentic collars, elaborately ornamented with raised ribs, alternating with cable and other patterns, in repoussé technique. Their terminal discs, which are attached by gold wire, are decorated with conical spikes surrounded by bosses, and groups of concentric circles. Similar motifs appear on 'bullae' or amulets of lead covered by sheet gold and on gold boxes perhaps used to contain cosmetics.

Although the greater part of the ornamental metalwork is in gold, some of the decorative motifs are also found on large bronze objects — concentric rings and bosses on the circular bronze shields, decorative rivets on the great riveted cauldrons. Some bronze weapons such as the spear-heads, rapiers and leaf-shaped swords are finished and elegant in form.

The art of the Bronze Age is an art of craftsmen, of metalworkers and reflects a society in which the development of trade and of specialised techniques were beginning to bring about change. Its objects of display and military panoply foreshadow the heroic age of warrior aristocracies whose culture marks the end of pre-history in the West.

11
12

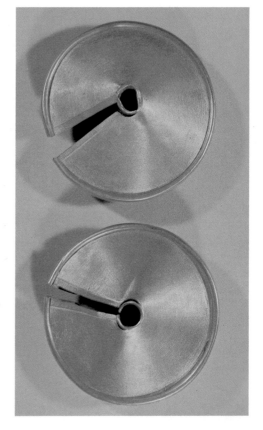

Early Celtic Art

11 *Gold dress fastener from Clones, Co. Monaghan. Late Bronze Age.*

12 *Gold lock-rings or hair ornaments from Gorteenreagh, Co. Clare. Late Bronze Age.*

It is not known when the Celts — that is, the people who brought the Irish language, came to Ireland. It may have been before the end of the Bronze Age. They were certainly here by the beginning of the Christian era and almost certainly for quite some time before that.

The evidence of archaeology goes to show that from about 300 BC onward, Ireland shared with Britain and many regions of the Continent many distinctive features of an Iron Age culture, which is named the La Tène culture, after a site in Switzerland. This was the culture which Caesar found in Gaul and Britain and from his testimony and that of other Classical writers, we know that it was the culture of Celtic speaking people.

La Tène peoples were iron-using agriculturalists, tribally organised with warrior aristocracies at their head. They occupied much of central and western Europe and their warlike expeditions brought them to Italy, where they sacked Rome in the fourth century BC and in the following century into Greece and Asia Minor. They migrated west and east but finally their power shrank under pressure from the north of the expanding Germans and from the south of the conquering Romans. By the end of the first century AD independent Celtic peoples survived only in Ireland, in mountainous regions of Wales and in part of Scotland.

The contacts of the Continental Celts were not only warlike. They carried on an extensive trade with the Mediterranean lands and imported, in particular, wine. This was one of the major influences on the distinctive art which they developed. They were especially skilled in metalworking and enamelling, they admired showy and fine metalwork and they treasured the wine-flagons and the wine-kraters which came to them from the Etruscans and the Greeks. These luxury goods — splendid drinking-vessels and table-ware — soon began to provide models for Celtic craftsmen but, from the beginning, the artists showed what was to be a constant feature of Celtic taste, their dislike of naturalistic and representational art. The artists of the Celtic world had different perceptions and different visual references from those of the Classical lands. They did not copy or represent nature but they may be said to have imitated it in some respects: every separate design is unique and perfect. Although repetitive they are not carbon copies but variations. They borrowed natural forms and turned them into semi-abstractions. Vegetable motifs — palmettes and tendrils — became spirals and running scrolls, human forms were stylised into masks. Celtic artists liked balanced compositions but avoided exact symmetry. They produced abstractions which always seem on the point of turning into organic forms; plants and animals which always seem on the point of turning into abstract geometry.

La Tène art is exceedingly homogeneous although it spans a considerable range of time and place. Certain themes persist throughout the centuries — animal designs which ultimately have an eastern origin, curvilinear forms, a love of colour, pattern and symbol. It is a non-monumental art — an art of personal display, glitter and brilliance but with an overall simplicity and restraint.

Some of the earliest examples of La Tène art in Ireland may be imports or copies of imports. This is almost certainly the case with a splendid gold collar found at Clonmacnoise which dates to about the third century BC and probably comes from Gaul. But by the 1st century BC, La Tène art is well established here. As is the case in Britain, much of the art is found on weapons or on the panoply of warriors. The Celtic warrior ornamented his weapons, his horse-furniture and his person and the decoration of these princely accoutrements reaches a high peak of perfection. Metalwork was the predominant medium and although iron was in use for weapons and tools, decorative metalwork still continued to be made in bronze and many personal ornaments in gold. The perfection of this insular art is perhaps due to the remoteness from the Classical world so that the Celtic imagination was given free rein.

The anthropoid sword-hilt from Ballyshannon (with stylised human heads) belongs to a type common in Britain and France and may have been imported

13

13 *Carved stone (cult monument) with La Tène curvilinear patterns, from Turoe, Co. Galway. Early Iron Age.*

14 *Bronze scabbard-plate with engraved ornament from Lisnacrogher, Co. Antrim. The design is of alternate spirals filled in with basketry patterns. Early Iron Age.*

15 *Gold collar from Broighter, Co. Derry, decorated with developed La Tène foliate patterns in repoussé, against an engraved background. Early Iron Age.*

16 *Roundel from bronze trumpet, Loughnashade, Co. Antrim, with late La Tène scrolls and peltae in repoussé technique. Early Iron Age.*

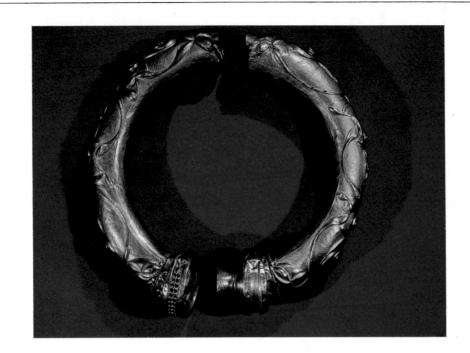

14
15
16

17

17 *'Petrie crown' — fragmentary mounting of bronze with chased ornament of bird-headed spirals and peltae. Find place unknown. Early Iron Age.*

18 *Two-headed Celtic idol, Boa Island, Co. Fermanagh. Early Iron Age.*

19 *Detail of bronze snaffle-bit with late La Tène curvilinear ornament from Attymon, Co. Galway. Early Iron Age.*

Early Celtic Art

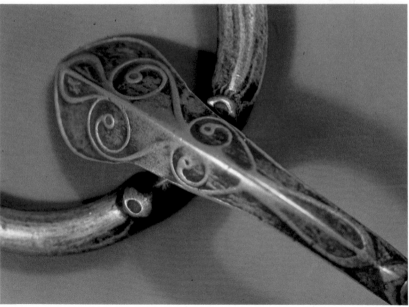

18
19

from Gaul or copied but the engraved sword-scabbards from Lisnacrogher, Co. Antrim are exquisite examples of the ability of the insular artists to handle curvilinear forms. Delicately engraved scrolls over-run the scabbard-plates, never monotonous, always fluid and inventive. A similar mastery of curved forms can be seen carved in stone, on the cult monument from Turoe, Co. Galway which unquestionably was carved by a native craftsman. It recalls some Gaulish monuments but the overall decoration of swelling curves, triskeles, spirals, carefully balanced yet assymmetrical, falls into the insular school of scabbard and mirror designs. It is a translation into stone of a plastic metalwork design — something that was to occur again and again in Irish art. There are other monuments in the same tradition at Castlestrange, Co. Roscommon and Killycluggin, Co. Cavan.

The finest example of the developed plastic style is the gold collar from Broighter, Co. Derry. Swelling trumpet curves, lentoids and spirals are set in high relief against a background of compass-drawn incised arcs which serve as a foil to the main design. A variety of techniques are used to produce these curvilinear patterns — the mainstay of the La Tène repertoire. Sophisticated compass-drawn curves ornament a series of bone-slips from Lough Crew, Co. Meath; openwork is used to great effect on two bronze boxes from Cornalaragh, Co. Monaghan and from Somerset, Co. Galway; and hatching and stippling of the background sets off the pattern on bronze spoons or castanets.

As time passed, forms became somewhat more symmetrical, as can be seen in the accomplished repoussé spirals and peltae which ornament the flange of the Loughnashade trumpet and on a series of circular bronze discs of unknown use, also ornamented with repoussé spirals. This period is known as ultimate La Tène and, although its beginnings seem to be about the first century AD, it is often difficult to be too precise in dating.

The most magnificent example of this stage of Celtic art in Ireland is the incomplete object known as the

Petrie Crown. It consists of a sort of frieze of D-shaped bronze pieces to which larger circular discs are attached, one of which still retains a conical horn. When complete, it might have been a religious object. All the pieces are decorated with low-relief patterns of spirals ending in stylized bird-heads, trumpet-spirals, peltae and studs of red enamel. The ornament was produced by chasing the surface of the bronze to leave the design in relief. On the cone the design was cut after it was in position. The extreme elegence and restraint of this object is in the best tradition of La Tène art although the peltae may suggest a latish date. The use of bird-head terminals to the spirals is a feature that was to survive for a long time in Irish art. Three hollow bronze cones in the Cork Public Museum are decorated in the same manner as the Petrie Crown and the chasing technique is used to produce a triskele design in relief on a small bronze disc from the River Bann now in the Ulster Museum.

Animal forms were a very important aspect of Celtic art and animals and birds played a major part in Celtic mythology. Although conventionally treated, often representations of animals have a surprising liveliness and naturalism, such as the little cult figure of a boar. More frequently, animal and bird forms, highly stylised, are used as part of a design or curved into a handle — a very ancient Celtic motif.

The human form, although it occasionally appears, is always more symbolically treated. It does occur in what are obviously Deities carved in stone, following in the tradition of Gaulish monuments. Most often it is the head or upper part of the body that is represented and this fits in with the Celtic preoccupation with the head as a religious or cult symbol. Most impressive is the two-headed Janus god from Boa Island, Co. Fermanagh, with highly-stylised faces in which eyes, nose and mouth form a pattern, the whole effect is of totally inscrutable power. A cruder three-faced figure comes from Donegal and a more finely carved, serene, three-faced idol from Corleck, Co. Cavan. Other heads now in Armagh Cathedral and a wooden figure in the National Museum all appear to be cult idols and are of interest in art terms only in showing how

completely the symbol dominates the icon.

The art of the Celtic craftsmen continued in Ireland on the fringes of a Britain dominated by the Romans although in a minor key. It can be traced on smaller objects — horse-bits and brooches. Many of the bits have elegant curvilinear patterns and often red champlevé enamelling. And the subtle modelling of bits and brooches such as the fibula from Navan, Co. Armagh, show how plastic skill survived. But the original impetus of the La Tène style could not last indefinitely, and although Ireland escaped the Roman invasion which finally eclipsed the Iron Age art of Britain, it needed new elements and influences to revitalise its art. The beginnings of the revival were brought about by increased contacts with the Roman world.

Roman Influence

A group of burials, with Romano-British gravegoods, found on Lambay Island off Ireland's east coast, gives evidence perhaps of refugees from the Roman conquest of Britain. At about the same time, we are told by Tacitus, Ireland's east coast was well-known to merchants from the empire. Contacts are attested by numbers of archaeological finds. By the third century there is increasing evidence of Roman influence in Ireland. In particular, types of dress-pin which were current in the military frontier zone and had distinctive British variants, began to be copied in Ireland. It is possible that at this time the non-Celtic Mediterranean costume of *brat*-and-*léine* (cloak and tunic) became the standard upper-class dress in Ireland. Pennanular pins or brooches came to be worn and these and other pins also of Roman derivation were used as vehicles for ornament. On them we can see the beginnings of the experiments which were to lead to a developed Christian art.

The art of this time is a jeweller's art of enamelling and miniature metalworking. Red enamelling was already known in Ireland in Iron Age times but now multicoloured effects were produced by the addition of plaques of millefiori glass to the champlevé enamel. Millefiori was made by drawing out thin rods of glass, fusing different coloured rods together in a bundle and again drawing them out into a single rod. Small slices were cut from this rod, revealing a multi-coloured pattern, and intricate and minute designs were produced by combining these. The technique was ultimately of eastern origin but was known to the Romans in Gaul and probably reached Ireland via Roman Britain about the second century AD. Certainly by the sixth century, millefiori was being made in Ireland. Workshops of glass-workers and enamellers have been excavated at Garranes, Co. Cork.

The simplest form of pin, known as a hand-pin, may go back in origin to the swan-necked pin of Iron Age times, but was modified and refined probably in northern Britain. In its earlier form the hand-pin had a circular head composed of three pellets in the upper portion and a lunated panel with simple curvilinear patterns in bronze set off by a red enamel background. Finally the panel was enlarged and the number of studs increased to five, each containing enamel. Hand-pins were being made from the third to the eighth century AD.

Pennanular brooches were derived from simple ring brooches with a gap in the ring and a short movable pin. Gradually the terminals were turned back and were given the shape of an animal head, in the old Celtic fashion, and the pin was lengthened. Later the brooches were cast with flattened and enlarged terminals to contain enamelled designs. Many of the developed zoomorphic brooches, as they are called, have elegant and graceful curvilinear patterns in true La Tène tradition. Often studs of millefiori glass are added which increases the colourful effect but in general does not improve the design.

The most elaborate and accomplished work in this style is found on mountings for bronze hanging-bowls. These bowls again derive from Roman types and were probably adapted for Christian use, possibly as hanging lamps but more likely as hand-basins suspended from tripods. Many have been found in Saxon graves but they were clearly of Celtic manufacture, although whether made in Ireland or Britain is a matter of controversy. These sixth - and seventh-century bowls had ornamental round or square escutcheons, decorated with increasing elaboration with patterns of running scrolls, peltae bird-headed spirals, in reserved bronze against red, yellow and blue enamel and later millefiori. Still later bowls, usually found in Viking graves in Norway, have escutcheons of various forms including bird-shaped and human figures, with angular patterns of red and yellow enamel and millefiori. These are undoubtedly of Irish origin and played an important part in working out patterns which were later translated into manuscript illumination. A button from Garranes, dress-fasteners known as latchets and other fragments display these same late Celtic curvilinear patterns, continuing the pagan metalworking tradition into the early centuries of Christianity. But it was undoubtedly the Christian church which was to provide the most potent Roman influence on Irish art.

The Christian faith came to Ireland from the Roman

Roman Influence

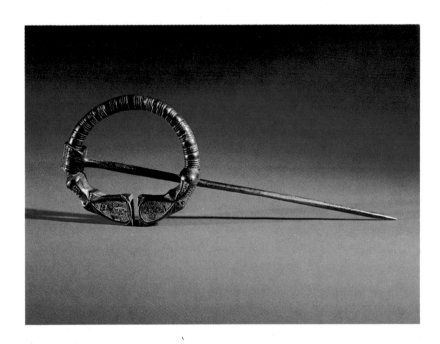

20 *Latchet or dress-fastener of bronze with ornament of spirals and peltae against a red enamel background. 6th century AD.*

21 *Zoomorphic brooch of bronze with settings of red enamel and millefiori c. AD 600. (Trinity College, Dublin)*

22 *Page from* Cathach *manuscript c. AD 600.(Royal Irish Academy).*

23 *Cross-inscribed pillar-stone from Reask, Co. Kerry. 7th century AD.*

Roman Influence

Empire (Gaul and Britain) and its influence on art may be regarded as a continuation of the process of Romanising. The first bishop, whose name was Palladius, was sent to the Irish Christians in 431 by Pope Celestine and was followed by other bishops, the most important of whom was St Patrick. By the middle of the sixth century Christianity was well-established. At about this time its character in Ireland began to be affected by the monastic movement, which had originated in the near-Eastern provinces. By the eight century, monastic organisation had almost wholly replaced the episcopal and diocesan organisation attempted by the first missionaries.

With Christianity came a repertoire of symbols such as the sign of the cross, the *Chi-Rho* monogram of Christ (widespread in Europe by the fifth century) and the images of the well of life or the True Vine. The Latin language, in Ireland as in western Europe generally, was the language of the Church and the use of writing, with Roman letters became common. Books were a necessary part of the equipment of the Christian Church. The first missionaries probably brought manuscripts with them and very soon they seem to have been copied in Ireland. By the sixth century, the Irish had not only developed a distinctive script — the Celtic half-uncial — but had begun to decorate the initials in a distinctive style. The earliest Irish manuscript, the sixth-century *Cathach* of St Columba, a copy of the Psalms, is preserved in the library of the Royal Irish Academy. Its script and initials are drawn in red and brown ink and the initials are ornamented with simple spirals and trumpet scrolls, such as we have seen on the hand-pins and brooches. Many of the initial letters are outlined with red dots, an oriental feature, and already the system of an enlarged initial followed by letters of diminishing sizes, has made its appearance. A fish or dolphin with a cross on its back ornaments another initial — this too is probably a Coptic motif.

The development of a distinctive lettering associated with the same range of Christian symbols may be observed also in the medium of stone. Among the primary monuments of Christianity are early Christian burial places and in many of these, there survive inscribed pillar-stones or slabs commemorating the dead. Such slabs and pillars with the *Chi-Rho* monogram or the Christian cross appear in all parts of Ireland. Initially these were simple incised crosses of the Latin form or the Greek cross-in-circle, but very soon influences from late La Tène metalwork are combined with the Christian symbols. Many of these monuments were not simply sepulchral, they seem to have been used as boundary marks, to signify the grave of the founder or simply as a symbol of Christianity set up in a prominent place in the monastic enclosure. Often the pillars remain crude and rugged (possibly descended from pagan standing stones) but spirals and knots and crosses of various forms, often with expanded terminals, are combined to produce elegant designs. One of the most accomplished is that at Reask on the Dingle peninsula.

The Golden Age

The early communities of Christian converts seem to have kept somewhat aloof from the pagan society around them and to have been more Roman in dress, hair-style and customs. Gradually their message was accepted. As the pagan kings, whose office was intimately connected with the old beliefs and practices, yielded to Christianity they seem to have favoured the monastic organisation which in Ireland became almost tribal in its character.

The monasteries were like villages, centred on graveyard and oratory, but with the dwellings of the community clustered around within the enclosure. The talents of the craftsmen were increasingly diverted to supplying the needs of these settlements. Small churches were required — at first simple rectangular buildings of wood, with an altar in the east end. Symbols of the new faith were erected, most notably the cross which was its chief sign. It seems to have been the custom from very early days to erect standing crosses over graves or on church sites. Books were needed for the Mass and other liturgical ceremonies — copies of the Gospels and of the Psalms especially. At first, no doubt, these were plain texts, but in time the Scriptures began to be treated as works deserving special reverence, and lavishly ornamented manuscripts were produced. The graves of the Christian dead, in the centre of the monastic enclosure, were treated with special reverence; specially honoured bones were enshrined, and small reliquaries became numerous. We know from St Patrick's writings that, from the very earliest days, offerings of jewels were made to the altars, and altar-plate, vessels, book-coverings and caskets were specially made. In time, wooden buildings were replaced in some cases by stone ones; stone grave-slabs and crosses show an increasing elaboration of sculptural ornament. Metalwork, manuscripts and stone sculpture shared a common ornamental style, which was influenced increasingly by the styles of neighbouring lands to which the monks, in penitential exile, travelled from the sixth century onward.

Metalworking

One of the commonest objects on the altars was a type of reliquary known from all parts of the Roman world: a small box or casket in the shape of a house with a gabled or hipped roof, a miniature version of a tomb, which was itself a miniature of a house or church. In Ireland, the box and lid were usually of yew-wood, to which were nailed bronze sheets, usually tinned or silvered and ornamented with settings of amber and enamels. Some of the shrines and fragments of them, have been found in Norwegian graves, having been brought back from Ireland by Vikings. One of the most interesting, the Moneymusk reliquary, is associated with St Columba, the Irish founder of Iona, and is in Edinburgh. It has on its silvered plates lightly engraved animal forms, reminiscent of Pictish carvings, and a broad-ribbon interlace against a stippled background. The shrines are associated with a seventh-century enamel style of Gallo-Roman derivation, in which the colours red and yellow predominate in champlevé panels, commonly of L-, T-, or cross-shaped settings. They also show signs of the influence of metalworking techniques of the Germanic world, notably the use of gilt bronze reliefs, usually interlaces, with sharply faceted surfaces which is known as *Kerbschnitt* or 'chip-carving', because of its source in wood-carving.

Ring-pins and penannular brooches continued to be the common dress-fastening, the terminals of the brooches becoming more elaborate. Then a change of fashion, probably in the seventh century, brought about the closing of the terminals to produce fully annular brooches. These, however, in the disposition of their ornament, retained a division which echoed the gap between the terminals of the penannulars; they are therefore referred to as 'pseudo-penannular' brooches. This development took place in Ireland; the western Scottish region (culturally almost indistinguishable from Ireland at this time) retained the penannular form in the highly decorated brooches of the late seventh and eighth centuries.

The most outstanding example of the developed Irish type is the so-called 'Tara Brooch' (actually found on the sea-shore near Drogheda) which is of silver, with linked terminals, richly and minutely decorated with gold filigree, animal ornament,

The Golden Age

24
25

24 *House-shaped reliquary known as the 'Emly shrine' from Co. Limerick, made of wood with silver plates and gilt-bronze and enamel mountings. c. 700 AD. (Museum of Fine Arts, Boston)*

25 *Tara brooch — Back, with ornament of gilt-silver bird - and animal - interlacing; copper spirals washed with silver and gold; and red and blue enamel studs with silver grid. c. AD 700.*

26 *Bronze belt buckle from Lagore, Co. Meath, with ornament of scrolls and trumpet-spirals. 7th century AD.*

27 *Silver chalice from Ardagh, Co. Limerick. c. AD 700.*

The Golden Age

28 *Kerbschnitt* spirals, trumpet-spiral patterns in
29 pierced silver foil against a red copper background, enamel, glass and amber studs, and carved and cast rim-reliefs of animals and human heads, all in the compass of a few centimetres. The brooch is equally richly decorated back and front and has attached to it by a hinge part of a length of silver trichinopoly cord. Even more elaborate and rich, although broadly in the same style, is the large two-handled chalice found in a deposit with other valuable objects near the bank of a rath at Ardagh, Co. Limerick. This too is mainly of silver and has a complicated construction involving many parts, with three main elements, bowl, stem and broad foot. There is a heavy rim moulding, under which is a richly ornamented band. Immediately below this, on the surface of the silver bowl, is a band of lettering, lightly engraved against a stippled background, with the names of the Apostles. The bowl is decorated with medallions, and the handles are richly ornamented with inlays and studs. The stem and the upper part of the foot have a glittering scheme of gilt *Kerbschnitt* spirals, frets, key-patterns and other motifs, while the underside of the foot is one of the most elaborately decorated parts of the chalice, with concentric rings of inlays and gilt bronze reliefs around a large crystal. The gold filigrees of the Ardagh chalice and Tara Brooch, while apparently derived from Germanic work, reach new heights of elaboration and minuteness.

Some reliquaries were not simply in the form of caskets to hold the relics but were made to the shape of the enshrined object. From an early date, the staves or croziers of holy men appear to have been given ornamental metal casings. At Moylough, Co. Sligo, a complete belt reliquary was found. The leather belt was encased in strips of bronze, with cover-mouldings hinged together. The metal casing is ornamented with inlaid medallions, and the form of buckle and counter-plate are carefully reproduced in decorative metalworking with silver spirals and enamels, although the reliquary buckle is non-functional. This object is in the late seventh- or early eighth-century style of the Tara Brooch and the Ardagh Chalice, but the ornament, although of fine quality, is less versatile and original.

28 *Ardagh Chalice, detail of handle and escutcheon showing enamel settings and studs and gold filigree interlacing.*

29 *Ardagh Chalice, Underside of foot ornamented with a rock crystal, amber, gold filigree animal ornament, kerbschnitt scrolls and blue glass studs. The outer ring is of silver with rectangular glass studs and panels of embossed silver and copper.*

30 *Bronze plaque representing the Crucifixion, from St John's near Athlone, Co. Westmeath; probably originally mounted on wood or leather, it may have been a book-cover. c. AD 700.*

31 *Mounting of cast bronze with enamel and millefiori from an Irish hanging-bowl found in a Viking grave at Miklebostad, Norway, c. 670 AD. (Historiska Museum, Bergen)*

The Golden Age

A small openwork gilt bronze plaque from Athlone 30 31 appears to have been a mounting originally fastened to a book-cover. It depicts the Crucifixion, in an iconography which became standard at the time in Irish work. Christ, clean-shaven is shown wearing a long robe, the body of which is decorated with low-relief spirals and frets. Two angels, with spiral-ornamented wings, support his head over the arms of the cross, while below the arms the central figure (much larger in proportion than the attendant figures) is flanked by the lance- and sponge-bearers. The face of Christ is stylised in the ancient Celtic manner and the whole scene is treated in the symbolic, unrealistic fashion which is a constant feature of early Irish art.

32 Manuscript Illumination

33 The eclecticism of the Irish artist and his contacts
with the Church in Britain and on the Continent are
seen best of all in manuscript painting and the
Columban monasteries of Iona and Lindisfarne
played a major part in the development of the
elaborate insular style. A number of manuscripts
from the library of Bobbio show some development
of the style of the *Cathach* and, in particular, one of
them shows the introduction of the carpet-page —
an entire page devoted to ornament. But the Book of
Durrow is far in advance of anything that has gone
before and illustrates all the influences and contacts
which helped to create the art of the Golden Age.

The Book of Durrow is a small manuscript of the
Gospels with pure Vulgate text and lavish
illumination. It was preserved for centuries at the
Columban monastery at Durrow and may have been
written there although certain features suggest a
Northumbrian milieu. The painting was done by an
Irish illuminator although the various motifs derived
from different sources can be seen separate and not
yet combined into a unified style. Each Gospel
begins with a carpet-page and a full-page symbol of
the Evangelist and there are elaborately
ornamented initials throughout the text. The colours
used are brownish-black, vermilion, yellow and
green. The Celtic element of the spiral, such as we
have seen developed on brooches and hanging-
bowls, appears throughout but there is one carpet-
page entirely covered with trumpet-spirals, peltae
and triskeles and bird-headed scrolls, more
elaborate than anything in metalwork. Also derived
from the jeweller's art is the symbol of St Matthew —
a stylised oblong figure with a robe of red and yellow
squares and polychrome patterns, directly copying
enamel and millefiori work. Another carpet-page is
composed of elaborate knot-work interlace, made of
broad ribbon bands bordered with a double contour
and this type of interlacing has its origin in the east
Mediterranean. Each of the symbol pages is
bordered with similar Coptic style interlacing. A
borrowing from Germanic art is the motif for another
carpet-page where elongated biting animals linked
in a continuous interlace are clearly based on
Anglo-Saxon metalwork. The frieze of animal

32 *Book of Durrow, fol. 2lv.*
Symbol of St Matthew.
c. AD 670.
(Trinity College Dublin)

33 *Book of Durrow, Opening of*
St Mark's Gospel.

34 *Book of Durrow, fol. 3v,*
carpet-page with trumpet
spirals.

34

35 ornament although very similar to animal patterns on such items as the jewellery from the Sutton Hoo treasure is treated in a more disciplined Irish manner. The animal symbols, eagle, calf and lion are related to Pictish animals but also to Saxon jewellery and the beautiful half-uncial script seems to have been an Irish invention. So here in this one gospel-book we see all the elements, Celtic and foreign, which combine to make the Irish style.

In the development after this initial stage, the borrowed ornamental elements were blended and harmonised. By the later seventh century, the Irish influence in Northumbria was beginning to be absorbed and replaced by new impulses from the Mediterranean. The style established in the middle of the century ultimately gave way to these influences. In the meantime, the splendid and luxurious Lindisfarne Gospels, painted at the end of the century, show that style at its finest. The Irish tradition is also traceable in fragments or in smaller and less luxurious books. The fragmentary Gospel books in Durham Cathedral Library, known as A II 10 and A II 17, show the absorption of ribbon animals into Irish, or Western mode, and the development of features such as the greatly enlarged and enriched capital letters. In particular, the *Chi Rho* Monogram of Christ, which introduces the genealogy in Matthew, became a field for ornamental fantasy, as may be seen for example in the handsome Welsh manuscript known as the Lichfield Gospels. Two large Irish books of the late eighth-century period, the St Gall Gospels and the Book of Mac Regol, are rather less richly ornamented but help to document the sequence which leads to the Book of Kells.

It is thought most probable that the Book of Kells, a sumptuous copy of the Four Gospels, was being completed at the Columban monastery of Iona when the first Viking raids began there, and that the book was then brought to the newly-founded Columban monastery of Kells, in central Ireland, shortly after AD 800, although this is not certain. The Gospel book is by far the most elaborate now surviving, with a majestic and beautiful text (in which perfection of visual finish was obviously regarded as more

5 *St Gall Gospelbook 51.
Figure of St Matthew. The
corners of the page depict
the symbols of the Four
Evangelists. 8th century AD.
(Cathedral Library, St Gall,
Switzerland)*

6 *Book of Kells,
Genealogy of Christ, fol.
201r. c. AD 800.
(Trinity College Dublin)*

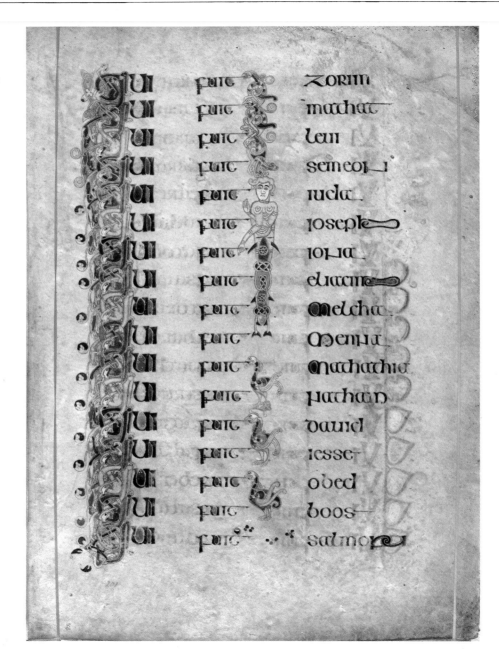

The Golden Age

important than accuracy of transcription) and an unstinting wealth of decorative embellishment, including a multitude of in-text sketches and miniatures as well as the set-pieces of carpet-pages, symbols and portraits of the Evangelists, full-page illustrations, fantastically ornamented initials (many occupying the full height of a page) and an array of formally decorative canon-tables and other guides to the content of the Gospels. The calligraphy and painting, finished with an enamel-like density on heavy vellum, appear to be the work of half a dozen or more persons, whose slightly different styles combine to give an impression of jewelled richness to every opening of the book. The work is intended to overwhelm with its minute perfection (a lens is needed to appreciate this quality) and with its luxuriance of colour. In this it succeeds. The account given by Gerald the Welshman (who came to Ireland with the Norman invaders at the end of the twelfth century) of a lost manuscript, the Gospel book of Kildare, can be applied without alteration to the book of Kells:

'Look more keenly at it and you will penetrate to the very shrine of art. You will make out intricacies, so delicate and subtle, so exact and compact, so full of knots and links, with colours so fresh and vivid, that you might say that all this was the work of an angel, and not of a man'.

37 Book of Kells, fol. 114r: The arrest of Christ.

38 Book of Kells, fol. 34r: Detail of Chi-Rho page.

39 Cross-slab Fahan, Co. Donegal, West Face. c. AD 700.

Sculpture

By the end of the seventh century, the inscribed pillar-stones, which were a common feature of the monastic enclosures, had lost their funerary character and had become more monumental, larger and more carefully shaped. A group of monuments in the Inishowen peninsula seem to illustrate the transition from cross-inscribed pillar to high cross proper. At Fahan Mura, a large slab, about nine feet high, carries on one face, a fine equal-armed cross of elaborate knot-work in bold relief and two stylised little figures. The other side has a similar cross. An inscription on the north edge of the *Gloria Patri* in Greek helps by the style of its wording to date the pillar to the seventh century. Nearby at Carndonagh is probably the earliest free-standing cross in Ireland. The shape is roughly hewn from the stone and the cross is covered on one side with interlacing similar to that at Fahan, while on the other there is an interlace cross above a simplified representation of the Crucifixion and three smaller figures. The cross is flanked by two small pillar-stones carved in the same style. The simplified figures and the knot-work interlacing with double contour line, are very similar to the ornament on the Book of Durrow and this regional group would seem to belong to the second half of the seventh century. The interlaced ribbon patterns and general appearance of these monuments seem to have been borrowed directly from Coptic Egypt.

The free-standing high cross was a well-established feature of most monasteries from the eight century on and frequently there was more than one cross. A plan in the eighth-century Book of Mulling in Trinity College Library shows a circular enclosure, the monastery, with crosses inside and outside, dedicated to various saints and evidently protecting the monastery. The ringed high cross or Celtic cross makes its first appearance. The finest monuments of the type are in the Slievenamon region along the lower Suir valley, and it seems clear that the ring around the head and other features derive from wooden and metal prototypes.

The two fine crosses at Ahenny, Co. Tipperary, the most striking of the group are covered all over with

The Golden Age

abstract patterns, spirals, frets and interlacings and studded with raised bosses, reproducing the ornament and form of wooden processional crosses sheeted in metal. The patterns are identical with those on eighth-century metalwork and even the technique of the carving of the sandstone is *Kerbschnitt* translated into stone. On the base of the crosses figure-sculpture appears, processions (including one with a ringed cross), hunting-scenes and strange animals, perhaps depicting some local event or having symbolic religious meanings. Similar crosses are found in western Scotland on Islay and Iona. Such themes of horsemen, hunting and curious animals, very similar to those employed on Pictish monuments, also appear on a group of rather later crosses associated with Clonmacnoise but there they are carved on the shaft and from about 800 AD figure carving begins to take the place of abstract designs.

The Viking Impact

40 *Grave slab, Clonmacnoise with inscription in half-uncials: a prayer for Tuathal Saer (the craftsman). 8th century AD.*

41 *North Cross Ahenny, Co. Tipperary, 8th century AD.*

Irish art in metalwork, illumination and sculpture had reached its full maturity by the end of the eighth century when the first Viking raids began. Since the monasteries were not only the chief patrons of the arts but also the major centres of population and wealth, they attracted the attention of the raiders. Island and coastal monasteries, in particular, became the victims of these hit-and-run pirate attacks in the first half of the ninth century. A later chronicler eloquently described '. . . *so that they made spoil-land and sword-land and conquered land of her, throughout her breadth and generally; and they ravaged her chieftainries and her privileged churches and her sanctuaries; and they rent her shrines and her reliquaries and her books.'* The truth of this account is borne out by the presence of many Irish objects in Scandinavian museums, carried off as loot in these early raids.

Soon, however, the Norsemen (who formed the bulk of the raiders on Ireland) began to establish permanent bases and trading posts along the coast, which were later to become the towns of Dublin, Cork, Wexford, Limerick and others. These settlements were the centres of far-flung trade which helped to bring new influences into Irish art. Excavations carried out in recent years in Dublin have revealed a great deal of the art and craftsmanship of the Viking town. Although Dublin and the other Viking towns stood somewhat apart from native Ireland, nevertheless close contacts were maintained. New markets were opened up by the extensive trade of the Vikings, bringing Irish artists into contact with England and Continental Europe. Viking animal styles began to appear in Irish art although usually in a distinctive and modified form. The use of silver became more common in metalworking as quantities of this metal were imported into the Viking ports, and a hybrid Norse-Irish type of art developed in the second half of the ninth century.

Pseudo-penannular brooches of Tara type continued to be made in the ninth century but now they are bolder in design and less minute in detail. The finest examples from this period, such as the Killamery brooch, are made of silver, tend to leave large areas undecorated and feature tubular - bodied marginal animals and brambling.

The most common type of brooch in the second half of the century and up to about 950 AD is the bossed brooch which is a characteristic Norse-Irish type. These brooches are always of silver and are truly penannular. Their characteristic decoration is a number of large bosses connected by bands which frame compartments with animal ornament. The animals are normally in the Scandinavian Jellinge style — rather disjointed ribbon animals with hatched or beaded bodies. Another hybrid type which became very popular in Scotland and Scandinavia is the thistle brooch, also penannular with spherical brambled terminals and a spherical pin-head. These again are always of silver and developed in Ireland in the late ninth century. Jellinge ornament again appears on some of the large examples. Pins and ring-pins of various forms in both bronze and silver are very common from this period and were used by both Irish and Vikings — many examples have been found in Dublin. An elaborate type is known as a 'kite' brooch from its large lozenge-shaped head which hangs from a very long pin. Both thistle and 'kite' brooches can be seen on a panel of Muiredach's cross at Monasterboice.

Trial-pieces of bone and stone bring us into touch with the workshops of the craftsmen. The early artists worked out their patterns and trained apprentices by scratching designs on animal bones and less often on pieces of stone. Finished designs are sometimes carved in bone and in these cases they may have been used to make wax moulds for bronze casting. A large number of such trial pieces has come from the excavations in Dublin and some of them illustrate remarkably the interaction between the Viking workshops and the Celtic monasteries. During the ninth and tenth centuries the production of reliquaries for bells, books and croziers became increasingly common. The decorative knops of croziers such as St Mels or the Kells crozier in the British museum are now usually divided into panels each containing animal ornament or interlace. *Kerbschnitt* and filigree have

42
43
44

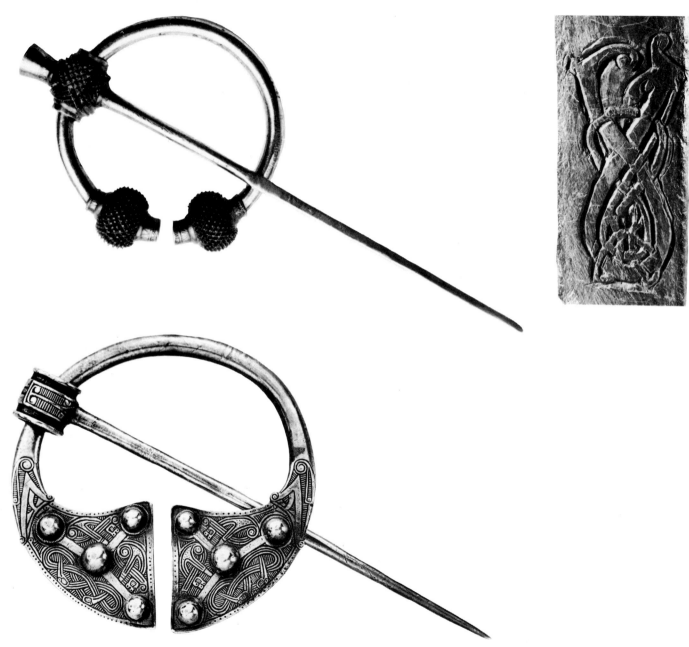

42 *Thistle brooch of silver: unlocalised find. Early 10th century.*

43 *Bone trial-piece, Christ Church Place, with animal interlace. 10th century AD.*

44 *Silver bossed brooch, Virginia, Co. Cavan. c. AD 900.*

disappeared but the panels may be coated with gold or silver and the animal patterns are bold and lively. A trial-piece from Christ Church Place has well-finished animal ornament almost identical with that on these 10th-century croziers. Another bone trial-piece from High Street has a Scandinavian Ringerike pattern which corresponds almost exactly with a panel on the shrine of the *Cathach*. This shrine was made probably at Kells by an artist called Sitric Mac Maec Aeda between 1072 and 1098. The Ringerike style, named from a site in Norway, is characterised by foliage patterns with loose lobed terminals and branching interlacing. It appears in Ireland in the second half of the eleventh century but soon assumed a characteristic Irish form where the tendrils acquired animal elements.

The destruction and plundering of the early raids seems most of all to have affected the art of manuscript illumination. The Book of Armagh was written in the early years of the ninth century. It contains historical material as well as a text of the gospels and, although there are some decorated initials and symbols of the evangelists in the tradition of the Book of Kells, it is a much simpler manuscript. After this for several centuries there is a virtual disappearance of decorated manuscripts. Many may have been destroyed by the illiterate raiders. A few psalters and hymnals come from the late eleventh century and have ornamented initials which show Ringerike influence. The Psalter of Ricemarch in Trinity College Library, which can be dated between 1076 and 1081, is the work of a Welsh illuminator and has rather stereotyped initials. The *Liber Hymnorum* also in Trinity and its companion hymnal in the Franciscan Library in Killiney, have elegantly drawn capitals of animal forms with foliate Ringerike details very similar to the metalwork of the period.

It was the art of stone carving that most of all flourished during the centuries of the Viking wars. From the beginning of the ninth century, scriptural scenes began to make their appearance mingled with the abstract patterns derived from metalwork. The Columban monastery of Iona may have played some part in this evolution for the ringed crosses of

Irish type in the west of Scotland have some intermingling of biblical scenes with abstract ornament on the shafts. The cross of Patrick and Columba at Kells, carved shortly after the monks from Iona had settled there in the early years of the ninth century, shows the same transitional style. As well as abstract designs of the Iona type on both faces, a number of scriptural scenes appear — Daniel in the Lions' Den, Adam and Eve, the Crucifixion. On one side the vine-scroll with birds and animals, so common a motif on Northumbrian crosses, makes one of its rare Irish appearances.

As the ninth century advanced, the Irish sculptors drew more and more on Carolingian ivories and frescoes for models of scriptural scenes which they transferred to monumental carving on granite and sandstone. There seems to have been a liturgical inspiration for a revived interest in these biblical scenes which were known earlier on fourth - and fifth - century ivories and sarcophagi. In particular a prayer for the dying, the *Ordo Commendationis Animae,* which was known in Ireland at about the year 800 and is preserved in a contemporary martyrology, provides a literary parallel for the scriptural crosses. In this prayer, God is called on for help and examples from the Old and New Testament are quoted — '*As Thou didst deliver Daniel from the Lions' Den', 'as Thou didst save the three children from the fiery furnace',* and these are the very motifs of the carvers. A group of crosses in the Barrow valley, in particular that at Moone, Co. Kildare, show a co-ordinated iconography. Now the shafts are divided into panels and the scriptural scenes are carved in a low relief. A charming simplicity is imposed by the hard local granite in which the crosses are carved and the old love of stylisation is apparent in for example the treatment of the twelve apostles at Moone which is more an arrangement of rectangles and ovals than any attempt at naturalistic representation. Abstract ornament and fabulous animals of Pictish type also occur but are beginning to be confined to the sides of the cross.

It is, however, on the fully developed scriptural crosses of the midlands, carved in sandstone that

The Viking Impact

45 the Irish sculptor shows his full powers. The finest
46 examples are at Monasterboice, Kells, Durrow and Clonmacnoise and they are architectural in proportion and composition and have an orderly sculptural scheme with scenes from the Old and New Testament on each face, carved in bold and rounded relief. There is nothing in the Europe of the time to compare with the cross of Muiredach at Monasterboice which is not only the most elaborate but the best preserved of the series. It is dated by an inscription to the early tenth century and this dating is confirmed by details of the ornament, dress and weapons. The cross is about eighteen feet tall and carries figure sculpture on the two main faces, east and west, and abstract ornament on the narrower sides of the shaft. The Crucifixion with angels, lance- and sponge-bearers occupies the central position on the east face with underneath panels containing scenes from the Life of Christ. The western crossing has an elaborate Judgement scene with Christ shown in the manner of Osiris from the Egyptian Book of the Dead, with cross and flowering sceptre. The damned are being prodded into hell on one hand and the just led to paradise on the other, while St Michael weighs the souls of the dead and Satan tries to upset the balance. Underneath are panels with Old Testament scenes. The whole iconography foreshadows Continental Romanesque but the details of Irish-type croziers, Viking swords and the gabled roof at the apex, as well as the ornamental panels set the cross surely in its Irish context. It seems likely that all these great Midland crosses are the work of one school of carvers.

For a time it seemed likely that this new interest in figural representation would become an important feature also of metalworking. On the book shrine known as *Soiscel Molaise,* which can be dated by an inscription between 1001 and 1025, vigorous carvings of the symbols of the evangelists and of a majestic figure, probably representing St Molaise, appear, as well as animal interlacements similar to those on the Kells crozier and trial pieces. A number of bronze openwork plaques represent the Crucifixion with lance and spongebearer in a manner similar to the high crosses and also have some foliate patterns of Anglo-Carolingian type. The

45 *High Cross Moone, Co. Kildare, detail with twelve apostles. 9th century AD.*

46 *High Cross Moone, Co. Kildare, Detail depicting Daniel in the Lions' Den.*

47 *Muiredach's Cross Monasterboice. East face showing Last Judgement. Early 10th century.*

48 'Breac Maodhōg', *Detail of book shrine showing female ecclesiastics. 11th century A D.*

49 'Breac Maodhōg', *Detail showing group of male ecclesiastics.*

50 *Crozier of the Abbots of Clonmacnoise. Late 11th century A D.*

bell-shrine known as the *Corp Naomh* is of several periods, the semi-circular crest which is the earlier part has a figure holding a book and horsemen and birds again in the style of the crosses. Even more elaborate figured scenes appear on the book-shrine known as the Shrine of the Stowe Missal. This again is of several periods but the main body of the shrine can be dated by an inscription to the mid-eleventh century. The shrine consists of an oak box with decorative silver plates. The applied panels include a hunting scene with man and animals, a warrior in profile with spear and rounded shield and a group of ecclesiastics in gilt bronze with bell and crozier on either side of a seated figure playing a lyre with a small angel above him. Similar rather massive figures ornament the shrine known as the *Breac Maodhōg.* This shrine has rows of male and female figures, presumably ecclesiastics or saints, in bold relief as well as a panel containing a seated harper.

But the excursions into representational scenes were short-lived and the Irish artist soon returned to the abstract patterns which were always his chief preoccupation and now they were given new impetus by influences from Scandinavian art. Although the metalworkers of this period never achieved the minute delicacy of the eight-century artists, some very impressive objects were made, which combined traditional techniques of bronze-casting, filigree and enamelling with innovations in silver and niello inlays. The Ringerike foliate style appears on the collar-knop of the Kells crozier in an elaborate silver and niello inlay and on two book-shrines, the *Cathach* and the *Misach,* associated with the monastery at Kells. The introduction of this style, as we have seen, probably came by way of the Viking settlement at Dublin but the pure foliage elements, although they occasionally survived into the twelfth century, were soon zoomorphised by the Irish artists. The later Scandinavian Urnes style (which takes its name from a church at Urnes in Norway) is based on a composition of quadrupeds and entangling wiry serpents and this free-flowing animal style was to achieve magnificent expression in Ireland in the art of the twelfth century. The splendid Crozier of the Abbots of Clonmacnoise, dating from the end of the eleventh century, shows

the subtle blending of Ringerike and Urnes styles. On the crook, a broad-band double-looped interlacing with free foliate ends made of silver with niello borders is inlaid in the bronze. The interlace has animal heads of Urnes fashion and is flanked by finer threads. The base of the crook is adorned with fierce cast animal heads of Irish Urnes style and the front has a grotesque human head; all are adorned with silver and niello. The knops are decorated with foliage and geometric panels set in enamel, confronted pairs of cast relief animals, and interlace. In beauty of design and technical excellence this crozier ushers in another peak period in Irish metalworking.

51
52

Romanesque

51 *High Cross Dysert O'Dea, Co. Clare. 12th century AD.*

52 *Kilfenora, Co. Clare 'Doorty' Cross. 12th century AD.*

53 *Kilteel, Co. Kildare, Romanesque capital. 12th century AD.*

54 *Nuns' Church, Clonmacnoise, Capital with Urnes ornament. 12th century AD.*

In the eleventh century, an administrative reform began to replace the long-established monastic organisation in Ireland with something more like the European pattern. As a result, bishops returned to prominence in the Irish church. The Ostmen or Viking towns opted out of the Irish ecclesiastical system and sent priests to Canterbury to be consecrated as territorial bishops. The movement extended to other parts of the country and reforming kings in Ulster and Munster supported the efforts to establish episcopal dioceses with fixed boundaries and sees. The change is reflected in the sculptural monuments from the late eleventh century onward.

Abstract ornament once again became all-pervasive on the high crosses, replacing the biblical scenes which had been the major themes of their decoration for almost three centuries. But a new element was now added which can best be seen on a group of limestone crosses in Co. Clare and on the Aran Islands. The cross is now treated as a crucifix with the figure of Christ in high relief occupying the upper part of one face of the shaft. Figures of bishops with croziers occupy also a very prominent place either in the upper portion of the other face or, as at Dysert O'Dea, Co. Clare, immediately below the figure of Christ. The figure of Christ is stiffly carved and wears a long robe while the bishops usually carry croziers of Continental type. Sometimes, as on the Doorty Cross, Kilfenora, other ecclesiastics — probably abbots — are placed in a subordinate position. As well as this high-relief figure sculpture, abstract patterns of frets, interlace and animal ornament appear on these crosses and the influence of late Ringerike and Urnes patterns is prominent. Similar iconography and decoration of Urnes animal interlacing appears about the middle of the twelfth century on crosses at Roscrea, Tuam, Glendalough and Cashel. At Glendalough the figure of Christ has the inclined head of Gothic iconography. The stone tomb carved at Cashel in the second quarter of the twelfth century has a pure version of the great beast and serpent combat theme in high relief, the clearest expression in Irish carving of an Urnes design.

The Romanesque style of architecture was

Romanesque

introduced into Ireland by one of the figures in the reform movement, Cormac Mac Carthaigh, King-Bishop of Cashel, when he built Cormac's Chapel on the Rock. This miniature masterpiece was consecrated in 1134 and while it retains many Irish features it has influences from England, France and Germany. The rich ornamentation of carvings includes chevrons and diaper patterns and an abundance of human heads, both realistic and grotesque. The chancel was originally decorated with wall and roof paintings but now only fragments remain. Many churches were built in the same style but soon the architectural features of the Romanesque were subordinated to an increasingly elaborate ornamentation, and at such places as Killeshin, Clonmacnoise and Clonfert, doorways and chancel arches are elaborately ornamented with abstract surface-patterns finely carved. These include chevrons of great variety, sometimes combined with animal interlacing of Urnes style, an abundance of stylised human heads, often with hair merging into Urnes animals or foliage. Much of the ornament has a graphic character more appropriate to manuscript or metalwork than to architectural forms. Figured scenes, so prominent a feature of Continental Romanesque and of the crosses of an earlier date, make only rare appearances — on a chancel arch at Kilteel, Co. Kildare and in a late church at Ardmore, Co. Waterford.

But the greatest achievements of the Irish artists in the twelfth century were undoubtedly in metalworking, and at this period there is a renaissance in this art, best seen on elaborate reliquaries, often dated by inscriptions. These inscriptions may now tell us not only the king or bishop who commissioned the work but the name of the artist who executed it.

Most of the finest objects were produced in the first quarter of the twelfth century. An early example, the shrine of St Patrick's Bell was made to the order of Donal O'Loughlin, King of Ireland, probably at Armagh between 1091 and 1105. Made of bronze, it is ornamented with silver-gilt openwork castings, gold filigree of great elaboration and millefiori glass studs. There are several variations of Irish Urnes animal patterns. On the sides, smooth rounded snakes form figure-of-eight designs and on the crest, large animal heads have manes of looser, freer interlace. One side of the crest has an Urnes version of the old Christian motif of the peacocks and tree of life. The openwork was elaborately executed by soldering together all the separate elements. While Scandinavian influence is apparent in details, the whole design is executed with Irish regularity and discipline. The most elaborate crozier from the period was made at the monastery of Lismore before 1113. It is ornamented with champlevé enamel studs in red, blue and white, panels of wiry animal interlacing with some Urnes influences and panels of human interlacing. The splendid arm reliquary of St Lachtin was probably made at Donaghmore between 1118 and 1121. It is an Irish example of a type well-known in Europe. It is made from sheets of bronze over a wooden core. The entire surface of the arm is covered with panels of orderly Urnes animal ornament inlaid silver bordered by niello. An openwork Urnes band divides the arm in two. The palm of the hand has a foliage pattern in silver, there are panels of silver filigree and the nails are sheathed in silver plates.

But the most accomplished products of this twelfth-century renaissance come from the west and the finest of these is the large processional cross known as the Cross of Cong made to the order of Toirdelbach O'Connor, King of Connacht at about 1123 to enshrine a fragment of the True Cross. The cross, of the Latin form, is made of sheets of bronze riveted together and outlined with silver tubular edging. The relic was protected by a large rock crystal set in a silver mounting in the centre of the crossing. The decoration in front is of cast gilt-bronze animal patterns, arranged in panels divided by silver bands and punctuated with glass studs and plaques of silver and niello. The back has an overall network of similar openwork animal interlace arranged symmetrically about the main axis. The animal ornament is the most perfect Irish version, orderly and disciplined, of the Urnes combat theme, the great beast enmeshed in figure-of-eight serpents. All the details are there: the pointed almond eyes and moustaches of the quadrupeds

54 *St Patrick's Bell-Shrine. c. AD 1100.*

and the loose ends of the serpents. The rivet-heads 54 have settings of red and yellow enamels in cruciform and step patterns. Great stylised animal heads bite the base of the cross and link it to a biconical knop also ornamented with animal interlace, below which a socket would have held a wooden staff.

Although it carries no inscription, the large bronze reliquary from the monastery at Lemanaghan, near Clonmacnoise (now preserved in the church at Boher, Co. Offally) is so similar to the Cross of Cong that it must have come from the same workshop. St Manchan's Shrine (as it is called) is a box of yew wood with gilt-bronze and enamel fittings, a variant of the house-shaped shrine in the form of a gabled roof.

The shrine stands on four solid feet but it could also be carried in procession and large movable rings are attached to the feet to take the poles for carrying it. The main ornamental scheme on both sides is a cruciform arrangement of five large bosses connected by short arms bearing enamels. The shrine was originally covered with silver plates traces of which remain here and there and against this background were placed a collection of small bronze figures eleven of which now remain. Magnificent animal patterns of great beast and serpent fill the bosses and the borders of the shrine as well as the triangular side-pieces. These side pieces, openwork mounted over gilt metal are the best preserved part of the reliquary. They have inner borders of engraved rather fleshy Urnes, and outer openwork borders. The red and yellow enamel patterns, the Urnes animal patterns and many other details link this shrine with the Cross of Cong and is also similar to the ornament on the Tuam market cross, also made under O'Connor patronage. The figures, which may represent saints or apostles, are all cast in one piece, naked except for short skirts which are all decorated, and close-fitting ridged sleeves. They seem to have been inspired by Continental Romanesque crucifix figures but are undoubtedly contemporary with the shrine — one has Urnes decoration on his skirt — and we might thus date the shrine perhaps a generation later than

Romanesque

55 the Cross of Cong but from the same workshop. The
56 animal ornament may also be compared with that on
an ivory crozier-head from Aghadoe now in
Stockholm which has a fine network of figure-of-
eight serpents and also a foliate Romanesque scroll.

These were the last masterpieces of the Irish
tradition in metalworking. The tradition in sculpture
and architecture survived, in the west of Ireland at
least, until the early 13th century, in spite of the
changes introduced by the Church reform and the
establishment of Continental monastic orders such
as the Cistercians. But by then, other major changes,
political and cultural, were associated with the
Anglo-Norman invasion, which began in 1169.

55 *Processional Cross of Cong, made to enshrine a relic of the True Cross c. AD 1123.*

56 *Detail Cross of Cong, ornamental knop with Urnes animal ornament and large animal head biting the shaft.*

57 *St Manchan's Shrine, Lemanaghan, Co. Offaly, now in the church at Boher. Mid 12th century AD.*

58 *Detail St Manchan's shrine showing boss with Urnes animal ornament and enamel settings.*

59
60

59 *Tomb effigy of Thomas de Cantwell, Kilfane, Co. Kilkenny. Early 14th century AD.*

60 *Silver-gilt chalice made in 1494 to the order of Thomas DeBurgo and Graunia Ni Maile. Similar in detail to the Lislaughtin Cross and possibly made in the same workshop, it is very close in form and decoration to a number of English chalices.*

The advent of the Cistercians and other Continental orders of monks initiated a period in which Irish art, coming under powerful influences from outside the country, became much less original and distinctive. This tendency was reinforced by the Anglo-Norman invasion. In architecture, the Early English style replaced the Romanesque in those areas initially occupied by the invaders: a good example is the parish church of St Mary at New Ross. The colonists even imported freestones from Somerset and elsewhere for their abbeys and churches, and completed works of sculpture were probably brought in as well to adorn them. By the 13th century, the imported styles and customs were being imitated throughout the country, and an Irish Gothic art had begun to develop.

A rather flat and stiff sculptural style (whose beginnings may be traced to the type of figure-carving on such twelfth-century works as the high cross at Dysert O'Dea) can be seen for example on the tomb-effigy of Conor O'Brien in Corcomroe Abbey, the relief of a bishop in the same abbey (which has a naive folk-art appearance), and also in the figures of bishops and abbots in the cathedrals of Kilfenora and Ardfert and Jerpoint Abbey. The military tomb effigies at Dungiven and Roscommon are good examples of the same style. The later development of this sculptural style may be traced in a very large number of sepulchral effigies, of which the large Cantwell effigy at Kilfane, Co. Kilkenny and the male and female figures now in the graveyard of the Church of Ireland cathedral at Cashel, Co. Tipperary are fine examples.

In metalwork, the change of style is first revealed through a debasement of the native tradition, a tendency towards repetitiveness and towards mass-production techniques, as in the Holy Cross book-mounting and more particularly, in the shrine of Dimma's Book where an openwork Urnes pattern has lost coherence, integrity and originality. The tradition has died away altogether by the beginning of the 13th-century, yielding largely, it would seem,to imported mass products, such as the enamelled cast-bronze crozier found at Cashel, one of a large number made from the same mould at

Limogues in the 13th century. The simple but elegant silver chalice and paten found at Mellifont may be of Irish workmanship but are in the style of 13th century English chalices.

The quantity of fine metalworking which has survived from the later Middle Ages is much less than from the pre-Norman period, possibly because the system of hereditary keeperships of shrines and other ecclesiastical objects did not apply in the newer foundations. However, we have some idea of developments from the additions and repairs made to early shrines in the medieval centuries. For the most part these show a deterioration both in technique and design and the methods used are quite different from the early work. Additions were often clumsily made, for example, the rock crystals applied to the shrine of St Patrick's Bell. Where the additions are more carefully disposed, as in the Crucifixion groups added to many shrines (e.g. the shrine of St Conall's Bell),they are usually conventional and undistinguished. Arcaded panels with standing figures, found in much of the later bronzework, for example the shrine of St Caillen, parallel the livelier designs of the late Gothic tomb- and altar-arcaded reliefs with figures of Apostles and saints, but the work in stone is on the whole more original and finer in execution. Occasionally, as in the cast relief figure-groups on the shrine known as the *Misach,* an old tendency to convert naturalistic forms into abstract decorative patterns may be observed. Engraved ornament combined with relief figures is a mannerism of this period and can be seen in the representations of groups of saints in the late work on the *Domhnach Airgid.*

Completely original work, as distinct from repairs and additions to ancient reliquaries, displays contrasting tendencies, sometimes, as in the Clogher cross, displaying a tendency towards revivalism of old styles and motifs, sometimes as in the Lislaughtin processional cross, being fully Gothic. The latter is a splendid object made by one William Cornelius with an expressive figure of the crucified Christ, openwork symbols of the evangelists and a lengthy inscription filled in with figures of birds and animals. By the end of the

Gothic

61 medieval period, with the establishment over most of the country of a stable and creative Hiberno-Norman society and culture, fine metalworking in a late Gothic tradition flourished, producing elegant and well-made chalices and other objects. Among the best surviving examples are the O'Dea mitre and crozier, commissioned for the Bishop of Limerick in 1418 and the silver 'de Burgo-O'Malley chalice' now in the National Museum. Pins, brooches, rings, ornamented weapons, ewers, pricket candlesticks and other metal objects, more or less ornamental, survive in some quantity from the Gothic period, but are in no way notably distinctive. As in the pre-Norman period, wood continued to be an important medium for the manufacture of everyday objects in Ireland and at the very end of the medieval period a distinctive type of four-handled drinking cup of wood, known as a 'mether' was developed. Wood was also used for works of art and a number of painted wooden statues survive from this period. These include Crucifixions, and representations of the Virgin and various saints and may be compared with similar works on the Continent. More interesting are the carved misericords in St Mary's Cathedral Limerick, dating to about the end of the 15th century. They are ornamented with figures and grotesque animals finely carved in black oak and are the only examples in Ireland.

The copying of manuscripts, including compilations of traditional learning and literature, continued throughout the medieval centuries. Ecclesiastical books were sometimes decorated with Gothic miniatures but the traditional compilations, such as the Book of Ballymote and Book of Lecan, often had decorated initials in which old styles of ornament, animal and interlace patterns, were, usually rather lifelessly, copied. But the great elaboration and the skill and virtuosity of the pre-Norman miniatures are no longer found.

The quantity and originality of late Gothic sculpture in stone (for example at Kilcooley and Holy Cross) testify to the vigour of the hybrid culture of late medieval Ireland, but that vigour tends to be attested more and more in the literary rather than the visual arts as Ireland enters the period of prolonged warfare associated with the Tudor conquest. The social and political upheavals which ensued, involving as they did the confiscation of land on a huge scale and the uprooting of the old system of patronage, introduced sweeping changes: and end to the polity of Gaelic Ireland and a beginning of the very different Ireland of modern times.

61 *Processional Cross, Lislaughtin, Co. Kerry of silver with floriated decoration and an inscription. Late 15th century AD.*

62 *Kilcooley Abbey, Co. Tipperary. Detail of tomb of Piers Oge Butler carved by Rory O'Tunney. Early 16th century AD.*

Gothic

Bibliography

Mitchell, Frank, *The Irish Landscape,* Collins, London 1976.

Harbison, Peter; Potterton, Homan and Sheehy, Jeanne, *Irish Art and Architecture,* Thames and Hudson, London, 1978.

de Breffny, Brian (editor). *The Irish World,* Thames and Hudson, London, 1977.

Harbison, Peter, *Guide to the National Monuments of Ireland,* Gill and Macmillan, Dublin, 1975.

Craig, Maurice, *Architecture in Ireland,* Department of Foreign Affairs, Dublin, 1978.

Treasures of Early Irish Art, 1500 BC to 1500 AD, Metropolitan Museum, New York, 1977.

Ō Riordáin, Seán P and Daniel, Glyn, *New Grange and the Bend of the Boyne,* Thames and Hudson, London, 1964.

O'Kelly, Claire, *Illustrated Guide to Newgrange,* English, John, Wexford, 1978.

Herity, Michael and Eogan, George, *Ireland in Prehistory,* Routledge and Kegan Paul, London, 1977.

Megaw, JVS, *Art of the European Iron Age,* Adams & Dart, Bath, 1970.

Finlay, Ian, *Celtic Art, an Introduction,* Faber & Faber, London, 1973.

Lucas, AT, *Treasures of Ireland, Irish Pagan and Early Christian Art,* Gill and Macmillan, Dublin, 1973.

De Paor, Máire and Liam, *Early Christian Ireland,* Paperback Edition, Thames and Hudson, London, 1978.

Henry, Françoise, *Irish Art in the Early Christian Period to AD 800,* Methuen, London 1965.

Henry, Françoise, *Irish Art during the Viking Invasions, 800-1020 AD,* Methuen, London, 1967.

Henry, Françoise, *Irish Art in the Romanesque Period, 1020-1170 AD,* Methuen, London, 1970.

Wilson, David, and Klindt-Jensen, Ole, *Viking Art,* Allen & Unwin, London, 1966.

Stalley, Roger, *Architecture and Sculpture in Ireland, 1150-1350,* Gill & Macmillan, Dublin, 1971.

Leask, Harold G , *Irish Churches and Monastic Buildings,* Tempest, Dun Dealgan Press, Dundalk, 1955-60.

Henry, Françoise, *Irish High Crosses,* Cultural Relations Committee of the Department of Foreign Affairs, Dublin, 1964.

Simms, G·O., *The Book of Kells,* Thames and Hudson, London, 1975.